SPOTLIGHT ON
NINETEENTH -CENTURY IMPERIALISM

Michael Gibson

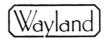

SPOTLIGHT ON HISTORY

Editor: Kerstin Walker
Consultant: Dr. M. Newitt, Department of History and Archaeology,
University of Exeter

Cover illustration: Watercolour of an incident during the Indian Mutiny,
artist unknown

First published in 1987 by Wayland (Publishers) Ltd
61 Western Road, Hove, East Sussex BN3 1JD, England

British Library Cataloguing in Publication Data
Gibson, Michael, *1936–*
Spotlight on nineteenth-century imperialism.—(Spotlight on history)
1. Imperialism—History—Juvenile literature
I. Title
325'.32'09034   JC359
ISBN 1-85210-086-9

Typeset, printed and bound in the UK at
The Bath Press, Avon

CONTENTS

1 NEW IMPERIALISM AND OLD

In the sixteenth, seventeenth and eighteenth centuries Europeans had acquired colonies to provide them with tropical products like sugar, tobacco, spices, tea, coffee and cotton. Colonial rivalries had led to frequent wars and the nineteenth century was to see an extension of these rivalries to all parts of the world.

Economic forces

All the Great Powers, Britain, France, Germany, Russia and the USA, were determined to extend their own territory and, where possible, to obtain overseas colonies. These countries were all at different stages along the path towards industrialization but they all required raw materials and expanding markets for their manufactured goods. The Great Powers often invested their own money in developing countries, helping them to build roads, canals, railways, mines, factories, ships and telegraphs.

Tea plantations such as this one in India provided the European peoples with luxury products at cheap prices.

The Royal navy, seen here in the English Channel in the early nineteenth-century, was the basis of British world supremacy.

Militarism

Intense rivalry between the Great Powers generated militaristic imperialism. On the one hand they felt driven to develop their armed forces to preserve themselves against attack; on the other, they required military might to enable them to expand. Between 1800 and 1900, the British fleet was so powerful that it could have sunk all the rest of the world's navies. Naval power was the basis of Britain's enormous overseas empire and caused great envy among her rivals, especially Germany. Army officers saw colonial conquests as an opportunity to further their careers and some of them rationalized their behaviour by referring to Social Darwinism. It was, they claimed, a law of history that only the strongest states could survive.

Internal problems

Governments also employed imperialistic policies to divert attention from their domestic problems, and to unite their countrymen around the nationalistic cause. The French, for instance, showed great imperial activity following the defeats of Napoleon I in 1815 and Napoleon III in 1870. The Russians stepped up their eastward expansion following their defeat in the Crimean War. The governments of weaker powers, such as Italy, strove to silence their critics by obtaining impressive colonies.

A missionary settlement in Africa. For some colonialists imperialism involved trying to convert local people to Christianity.

Overpopulation

Overpopulation, real or imagined, was another reason for expansion. The population of Europe was rapidly expanding throughout the nineteenth century. Most governments feared this would bring economic and political disaster. How, they asked themselves, could they feed and employ all these extra people? From the beginning, many new colonies like Australia and New Zealand were regarded as resettlement areas for 'surplus' citizens.

A sense of mission

Some imperialists had a genuine sense of mission. Christian missionaries wanted to take their religion to heathen peoples. The anti-slavery groups saw imperialism as a means of stamping out the slave trade. Some idealists believed it was their duty to provide 'primitive peoples' with the benefits of 'modern civilization' – medicine, education and law and order.

Each move to acquire colonies had varying and complex reasons. Hopes of economic gain were important in making the initial decision to colonize, but once colonies had been acquired other forces began to take over. The most pressing concern was to defend the territories against rival claims and to consolidate the authority of the colonizing power. It was this need, more than any other, that obsessed the Great Powers once they had embarked on an imperialistic programme.

2 THE EUROPEAN POWER STRUGGLE

For centuries, even before the French Revolution of 1789 which resulted in the overthrow of the French monarchy, Europe was convulsed by dynastic struggles. The emperors, kings and princes attempted to increase the size of their empires by marriage and war. Britain was ruled by the Hanoverians; the Netherlands by the House of Orange; France, Spain and Southern Italy by the Bourbons; Austria-Hungary by the Hapsburgs; Russia by the Romanovs; and Turkey by the Ottomans.

The Treaty of Vienna of 1815, which brought to an end the Napoleonic Wars, was an important territorial settlement that was to have a lasting influence on Europe for nearly fifty years. At that time Germany was a patchwork quilt of independent states and territories,

The Congress of Vienna agreed a territorial settlement for the European powers that was to last for fifty years.

which both the Hohenzollerns of Prussia and the Hapsburgs of Austria hoped to add to their dominions. Italy also consisted of a mixture of powerful and petty states dominated by the Hapsburgs, Bourbons and the rulers of Sardinia-Piedmont.

The French Revolution encouraged the spread of nationalistic ideas. The revolutionaries not only destroyed their own monarchy and replaced it with a republic but set up republics in the Netherlands, Switzerland and Italy. Even though these new states were soon swallowed up by the Napoleonic empire, the peoples of Europe felt a new sense of identity.

Nationalistic revolts
Following Napoleon's overthrow, the old ruling families tried to revert to the status quo which had existed before the Napoleonic Wars. However, a series of risings forced them to admit that they had entered a new age. In 1820, for instance, the Spanish Bourbons were able to put down a popular rising only with French help. When the people of the Two Sicilies (Naples and Sicily) rose in revolt, the Austrians had to intervene to prevent the Bourbons being overthrown. Successful nationalist risings against the Turks took place in Serbia and Greece.

At the Congress of Troppau in 1820, the European rulers decided that the way to halt the spread of nationalism was to establish a system of mutual co-operation and intervention among states, under which disputes would be settled through consultation and agreement. 1830, however, witnessed another series of revolts. In France, Charles X, the last Bourbon king, was replaced by Louis Philippe. In 1832 the Netherlands separated into Holland and Belgium. The Austrians, however, succeeded in suppressing a series of risings in Italy although the Young Italy movement led by Guiseppe Mazzini (1805–72) continued to grow in popularity. Unrest in Germany drove the rulers of Saxony, Hanover, Brunswick and Hesse-Kassel to grant their people parliaments and in consequence added to the strength of the Young Germany movement led by Heinrich Heine (1797–1856). A rising in Warsaw was ruthlessly suppressed by the Russians.

1848 Revolutions
Although there was a growing demand by middle-class liberals for reforms to guarantee civil rights and to promote industrial and commercial development, for a long time the European rulers were able to hold them and the nationalists in check. Then, in 1848, Louis Philippe was expelled from France and the short-lived Second Republic held sway from 1848 to 1852. Serious disturbances in Italy forced the rulers of Sardinia-Piedmont, Tuscany, the Papal States and the Two Sicilies to grant constitutions. Indeed, Charles Albert of Sardinia-

1848 was a year of revolution throughout much of Europe. The picture shows Italian nationalists attacking the Papal Palace in Rome.

Piedmont seized the opportunity to attempt to unite Italy but was defeated by the Austrians at the Battle of Custozza and had to abdicate in favour of Victor Emmanual II. Further risings in Naples and Venice were crushed.

An attempt to unify Germany also failed. The Frankfurt Constituent National Assembly put forward ideas about unifying Germany but had no powers to implement them. Although Frederick William IV of Prussia thought it politic to grant his people a constitution, he remained in firm control of the situation. In Austria a rising in Vienna brought about the abdication of the Emperor Ferdinand I in favour of Franz Josef (1848–1916), who with Russian help put down risings in Austria, Hungary and Bohemia.

Unification of Italy

During the 1850s and 1860s Europe rapidly industrialized and the need grew to unite the small states of Germany and Italy under an efficient and modern administration. In 1859, Napoleon III of France (1852–70) helped Victor Emmanuel of Sardinia to defeat Austria and add Lombardy to his dominions. Meanwhile, Guiseppe Garibaldi liberated the Two Sicilies and then handed them over to Victor Emmanuel. Shortly afterwards, the peoples of Parma, Modena and Tuscany decided to unite with Sardinia. In March 1861, Victor Emmanuel was able to proclaim himself King of Italy.

The National Liberals dominated the Frankfurt Constituent Assembly of 1848; one of their main demands being the unification of Germany.

Garibaldi with Victor Emmanuel. Garibaldi's capture of the Two Sicilies enabled Emmanuel to proclaim the unification of Italy.

Franco-Prussian war
The struggle to control Germany continued during this period. Napoleon III hoped to obtain the Rhineland when Austro-Prussian rivalry finally resulted in war. However, to the French emperor's astonishment, the Austro-Prussian war in 1866 lasted only seven weeks, leaving the Prussians as the undisputed victors. Napoleon III felt cheated and tried to reach an agreement with Otto von Bismarck, the wily Chancellor of Prussia. The emperor was outmanoeuvred and declared war on Prussia in 1870. The French armies were convincingly defeated, Napoleon abdicated and in 1871 the German Empire was proclaimed in the famous Hall of Mirrors in the great French Palace of Versailles. This established Germany as an important land power.

The creation of the German Empire, proclaimed in 1871, brought about a major shift in the balance of power in Europe.

Colonization

Between 1871 and 1914, the European Powers largely satisfied their desire for wealth and territory by partitioning Africa and the Far East. During the same period, the USA survived a cruel Civil War (1861–5) and extended its frontiers westwards from the Mississippi to the Pacific, while the Russians expanded eastwards from the Ural mountains to the Pacific. Although much attention was directed at imperial expansion, considerable tension still existed in Europe itself between the Great Powers. Bismarck, particularly, feared that the French would seek revenge for their defeat in 1870–71 and so built up a system of military alliances, which, after his death in 1898, divided Europe into two 'armed camps'. On the one side, there were the Central Powers (Germany, Austria, Italy and Bulgaria) and on the other the Allies (France, Russia and a very reluctant Britain).

Between 1900 and 1914, the arms race led to a series of 'incidents' between the Great Powers, which generated an atmosphere of hostility in Europe. The struggle for power eventually resulted in the outbreak of the First World War (1914–18).

Map showing the partition of Africa in 1914.

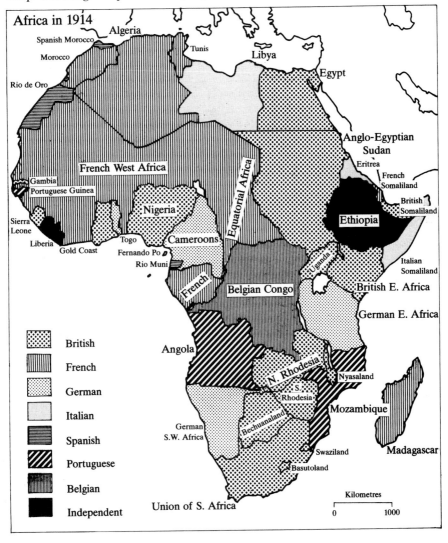

3 THE SCRAMBLE FOR AFRICA

Africa with its gold and slaves had been the target for European greed since the fifteenth century. In the nineteenth century, industrialists in Europe and America wanted new markets and prepared to force other countries to trade with them. After 1875 economic depression forced the industrialized states to compete with each other for raw materials and markets. Attention was focused on Africa, which was becoming more accessible following the opening up of the interior by explorers such as Livingstone and Stanley.

An African slave market. Slaves provided Europeans with cheap labour to work on their colonial plantations.

The opening of the Suez Canal in 1869 meant that shipping between East and West could avoid the journey around Africa's Cape of Good Hope.

The conquest of North Africa

At the beginning of the nineteenth century, most of North Africa was still part of the Ottoman Empire. In 1830, however, the French occupied Algeria. This attractive country became France's granary and a major area of white settlement. The French also hoped to increase their influence in Egypt by supporting Mehemet Ali, the Ottoman governor, who seized power for himself and tried to conquer Syria. However, Britain supported the Turks, and Mehemet Ali had to withdraw. In spite of this setback, it was French capital and expertise that built the Suez Canal between 1859 and 1869. However, in 1875, Benjamin Disraeli, the British Prime Minister, bought a majority of the Canal Company's shares despite French protests. A nationalist rising in Egypt in 1882 provided an excuse for the British to occupy and take over control of the country.

The French, however, obtained some compensation by establishing a protectorate over Tunisia in 1881. France's success in turn infuriated the Italians who had been hoping to expand into this area. When the French occupied Morocco in 1911, the Italians were able to obtain some belated compensation by taking Tripoli from the Ottoman Turks, but only at the cost of a bloody war (1911–12). Thus, by 1914, the whole of North Africa was in European hands.

The Fashoda Incident

Equatorial Africa fell to the French. Starting from their base in Senegambia, French explorers moved steadily eastwards across the savannas. Between 1854 and 1865, General Faidherbe created a highly efficient force of African troops with which to suppress the tribes in the interior. Gradually, the Sahara and the Western Sudan were 'pacified'. Once again, the British intervened to prevent the realization of a French plan of further expansion. In 1884 General Gordon was sent to relieve the garrison at Khartoum. The massacre of Gordon and the garrison by Sudanese rebels in 1885 shocked the British. In 1896–8, General Kitchener led a punitive expedition into the Sudan. No sooner had a French party led by Major Marchand arrived to claim the area than they found themselves confronted by an overwhelmingly powerful British force. For a time it was feared that the Fashoda Incident would lead to war between the two Great Powers. In the end,

Kitchener confronting Marchand at Fashoda in 1898. A crisis over colonial rivalry was avoided only through the French backing down.

Britain's capture of the Cape of Good Hope in 1806 gave her a firm foothold in southern Africa.

however, the French backed down. In the meantime, the Italians took over Eritrea (1887–90), Ethiopia and Somaliland (1889). In 1894–6, the Ethiopians rose against the Italians and defeated them at the Battle of Adowa. Not until 1936 was this humiliation wiped out when Mussolini invaded and conquered the country.

Tropical Africa was divided between the French, British, Germans and Belgians. In West Africa, the initial work of the British Niger Company was completed by Lord Lugard, who established peaceful government in Nigeria in 1893. Meanwhile, the British East Africa Company exploited Kenya and Uganda. Once again, Lord Lugard was asked to establish a protectorate over the two areas. At the same time, the Germans occupied Togo and the Cameroon (1884) in West Africa, and Tanganyika (1886) in East Africa. During the same period, King Leopold of the Belgians made himself master of the Congo in West Central Africa.

South Africa
At the beginning of the nineteenth century, there were only three European colonizers in South Africa: the Portuguese, British and Dutch. The Portuguese owned Angola and Mozambique, and the British seized Cape Colony from the Dutch in 1806. Many of the original Dutch settlers, the Boers, objected to British rule and moved north into the interior. This 'Great Trek' (1836–44) led to the foundation of the Orange Free State in 1852 and the Transvaal in 1854. At the same time, the British occupied the rich province of Natal. Britain

wanted to dominate South Africa, and decided to achieve this by annexing the Transvaal and by conquering the Zulus, the most powerful independent black peoples. However, the defeat of the British by the Zulus at Isandlwana destroyed their military reputation and the Boers, unimpressed by the British victory over the Zulus at Ulundi, took up arms to regain their freedom. The British suffered a series of defeats during the First Boer War of 1880–81 and had to recognize the independence of the Boer republics.

British interest in Central Africa can largely be explained by the country's mineral wealth. In 1870, diamonds had been discovered in Griqualand. In spite of Boer competition, the British persuaded the chief of the Griqua tribe to apply for inclusion in the British Empire and the area became a British Colony in 1872. One of those who made his fortune was Cecil Rhodes, whose main ambition was to extend British control over Central Africa and to gain access to the sea for his extensive British mining operations. Between 1889 and 1893 his British South Africa Company established control over Northern and Southern Rhodesia.

The 'Great Trek' by the Boers into the African interior led to the formation of the Orange Free State and the Transvaal.

The vast reserves of gold in South Africa provided the colonizing powers with one of the richest natural resources in the world.

In 1886 gold had been discovered in the Transvaal. The Boers were farmers and not interested in mineral wealth, so they allowed foreigners (Uitlanders) to exploit this rich resource. But the Boers taxed the foreign miners without allowing them any political rights. As unrest grew, Rhodes saw an opportunity to topple the Boer government and restore British rule. Dr Jameson, one of Rhodes' friends, collected a force in Rhodesia and rode into the Transvaal in 1895, expecting the Uitlanders to join him. In fact, this did not happen: Jameson's force was surrounded and disarmed, and Rhodes' political career was ruined.

The Second Boer War
Britain's concern for the future of the gold mines and her own supremacy in the area led to the Second Boer War of 1899–1902. At first, the British forces suffered serious defeats, to the unconcealed delight of the other Great Powers. Gradually, however, Boer resistance was overcome by dividing up the country with barbed wire fences

Britain's defeats in the Boer War damaged her prestige among the Great Powers.

protected by blockhouses. Boer women and children were placed in concentration camps where 20,000 died of disease. This brutal war ended in 1902 with the Treaty of Vereeniging, by which the Boers lost their independence. However, in 1910, political independence was regained when dominion status was granted to the Union of South Africa by the British.

From the European point of view, 'the Scramble for Africa' had been an attempt to share out the wealth of the continent between competing industrial economies, and it had been achieved without recourse to war between the Great Powers. For the Africans it had meant forced labour, taxation, the ravages of epidemics and the humiliation of military defeat. These years built up a bitter legacy of anger among many of the colonial peoples, which independence has failed to remove.

4 MANIFEST DESTINY

In 1800, North America was divided between the new United States, British Canada, French Louisiana and Spanish New Spain. Then, in 1803, the USA bought Louisiana from Napoleon I and doubled its size overnight. President Thomas Jefferson was anxious to establish his country's claim to the Northwest and sent Meriwether Lewis and William Clark to blaze a trail there. After many adventures among the Indian tribes, they sighted the Pacific Ocean on 7 November 1805. Winning the West was, according to some historians, the key experience that moulded the American nation.

Winning the West

The way was led by fur trappers and buffalo hunters. Gradually, these frontiersmen made their way across the Great Plains and up into the foothills of the Rocky Mountains. After the hunters and trappers came the settlers, whose numbers were swollen by mass emigration from Europe. During the 1840s, increasing numbers of wagon trains set out for the well-watered, wooded valleys and hills of Oregon. While these

Emigrants halting on their long trek to settle in the American West. Thousands made this journey in the 1840s.

settlers were tilling the virgin soils of the Northwest, the religious leader Brigham Young led a party of Mormons across the Rockies and founded Salt Lake City, Utah in 1847. In spite of the formidable difficulties presented by the journey, thousands of people tramped the 2,413 km (1,500 miles) from St Louis to Salt Lake City.

Frontiersmen also pushed south into Texas, which was then a no-man's land between Spanish Mexico and the USA. The first American settlers grew corn, sweet potatoes and cotton – at first, cattle ranching was only a sideline. In 1836, General Santa Anna, the dictator of Mexico, moved into Texas and besieged the tiny American fort at the Alamo. There 187 men led by Davy Crockett and Jim Bowie sacrificed their lives to slow the dictator's advance. In the time they bought with their lives, General Sam Huston was able to create an army which defeated Santa Anna at the battle of San Jacinto. In 1845, the Texans voted to join the USA. When the Mexicans heard the news, they declared war, but were defeated at Buena Vista in 1847. The ensuing peace treaty in 1848 gave the USA the territories of Texas, Arizona, New Mexico, Colorado, Utah and California.

A meeting of Mormons in Salt Lake City, the destination for many of the settlers in the USA.

The bloody defence at Fort Alamo was a fine example of the courageous spirit of the Americans.

The forty-niners

Before the discovery of gold in the River Sacramento in 1848 California had attracted only a small number of settlers. Following the discovery in 1849, thousands of 'forty-niners' crossed the Plains or sailed round the Cape to seek their fortunes. The overland trails were soon marked out by lines of crosses and heaps of animal bones – one observer counted the carcases of 350 horses, 280 oxen and 120 mules in the space of 24 km (15 miles). Soon, however, stage coaches were crashing and rattling their way across the Plains. Wells Fargo transported goods from the east coast right across to California, while Pony Express riders carried messages over the same distance. The newly acquired lands attracted massive capital investment and not long afterwards, stage coaches and roughriders were replaced by railroads and the telegraph. The first transcontinental telegraph was completed in 1861. A year later, the Union Pacific Railway Company started to lay track westwards while the Central Pacific Company built eastwards. On 10 May 1869, the two lines were officially united and 'the Iron Horse' reigned supreme.

The Sand Creek Massacre

Until this time, the Sioux, Cheyenne and Comanche Indians had lived on the Great Plains. These great tribes deeply resented the activities of the buffalo hunters and settlers. Worse was to follow when gold was discovered in Montana in 1863. Wagon trains of prospectors continually rolled across the Plains only to be ambushed by the Indians. Shanty towns grew up along the trails, which were guarded by forts garrisoned by the American army. Relations between the Indians and the whites quickly deteriorated. The Sand Creek Massacre of 1864, at which a group of white irregulars massacred Chief Black Kettle's tribe, marked the beginning of the Sioux Wars. Thereafter, every wagon

The discovery of gold in 1848 brought thousands of people to California to seek their fortunes.

A photograph showing the joining of the Union Pacific and Central Pacific Railways, which linked eastern and western USA.

train was attacked by Chief Red Cloud's Sioux. The American cavalry, newly armed with Springfield-Allen repeating rifles, inflicted a terrible defeat on the Indians at the Wagon Box Fight in 1867 and Red Cloud was forced to make peace in 1868. He was assured by the president of the USA that the Sioux would be allowed to keep their traditional lands for ever.

Not long afterwards, however, gold was discovered in the Black Hills and the government tried to force the Sioux to sell the land. The Indians refused, because as their Chief Crazy Horse said, 'One does not sell the earth upon which the people walk'. The government ordered the 'hostiles' into reservations, but many of the Sioux met in council at the Little Bighorn (1876). When General Custer and the Seventh Cavalry attacked their camp, they were cut to pieces. The whole of white America was deeply shocked and the Sioux were rounded up and forced on to reservations.

29

American imperialism

On achieving independence, the USA had made it clear, in the Monroe Doctrine, that they would not allow other powers to interfere in the internal affairs of the Americas. It was hardly surprising, then, that when the people of Spanish Cuba revolted in 1895, many Americans longed to join them in their struggle for freedom. President Cleveland, however, refused to intervene until the US battleship *Maine* was blown up in Havana harbour in 1898. When the Spanish refused to accept an offer of American mediation, war was declared and an American expeditionary force landed in Cuba and defeated the Spanish forces. As a result, Spain was forced to cede Cuba, Puerto Rico and the Philippines to the USA. By a curious twist of fate, the fiercely anti-imperialist Americans found themselves in control of a colonial empire.

American settlement of the West led to conflict with the tribes of Indians living on the Great Plains.

The construction of the Panama Canal enabled traffic between the Atlantic and Pacific Oceans to avoid the journey around Cape Horn.

Dollar diplomacy

For many years, the Americans considered the possibility of cutting a canal linking the Atlantic and Pacific Oceans through the isthmus of Panama. Indeed, in 1889, Ferdinand de Lesseps, engineer of the Suez Canal, spent vast sums in an unsuccessful attempt to do just that. In 1903, President 'Teddy' Roosevelt decided the time was ripe for such a venture. When the Columbian government, the rulers of Panama, proved to be unco-operative, Roosevelt engineered an 'uprising' and promptly recognized the Republic of Panama. In August 1914, the Panama Canal was opened to commercial traffic and the difficult journey around Cape Horn at the southernmost tip of South America was no longer necessary.

Not only did American presidents 'speak softly and carry a big stick', they succeeded in controlling the Americas by means of 'dollar diplomacy'. By investing heavily in their neighbours, they made them economically dependent.

During the course of the nineteenth century, the USA not only succeeded in adding the West to their territories, but also bought Alaska from the Russians in 1867 and established a remarkable economic and political ascendency over North and South America. By 1914, they were ready to become the world's greatest power.

5 THE DOMINIONS

One of the most important consequences of the rise of the British Empire in the nineteenth century was the success of its great dominions: Canada, Australia and New Zealand.

Although the thirteen American colonies obtained their independence in 1783, Canada remained British. In 1791, William Pitt's Act divided the colony into Upper Canada (now Ontario) and Lower Canada (now Quebec). Each province elected an assembly although real power remained in the governor's hands. By 1815, discontent was widespread. The original Roman Catholic French settlers of Lower Canada objected to the favour shown to the new British immigrants. In Upper Canada, incoming settlers quarrelled with the 'Family Compact', which was the ruling oligarchy established in this area at the end of the eighteenth century. The people of both provinces wanted a more democratic form of government.

Lord Elgin in the Canadian parliament giving the royal assent to bills passed by the legislature.

The vast open plains of Canada provided large quantities of wheat for Britain.

The Durham Report

Rebellions broke out in both provinces in 1837. Louis Papineau and the French party in Lower Canada and William Mackenzie and his followers in Upper Canada announced their independence. Both risings were put down easily enough and Lord Durham was sent to Canada as High Commissioner. His famous report included recommendations that the two provinces be united and that the Colonial Executive be made responsible to an elected assembly. The provinces were united in 1840 and Lord Elgin, Governor-General from 1847 to 1854, saw to it that the Canadian prime minister and cabinet were responsible to the Canadian Parliament.

While the French Canadians feared they would lose their identity, other Canadians like the people of the Maritime Provinces (Nova Scotia, Prince Edward Island and New Brunswick) demanded closer ties with each other. The British North America Act of 1867 made Canada a federation ruled by a parliament with upper and lower houses. In 1842, Britain and the USA agreed to partition the North American continent, and more and more provinces joined the federation: Rupert's Land and the North West Territory (1870); Manitoba (1870); British Columbia (1871); Alberta (1905) and Saskatchewan (1905).

33

The Red River Rising

The new dominion was threatened by the Red River Rising in 1870. Louis Riel, a young French Canadian, seized Fort Garry on the Red River and proclaimed himself president of the Republic of the North West. As soon as the self-declared 'president' heard that a punitive expedition was on the way, he fled to the USA. The work of unification was greatly helped by the construction of the Canadian Pacific Railroad (1873–86) which crossed the continent from the Atlantic to the Pacific coast and opened up the Great Plains to farmers. Following this, Canada was to become the main exporter of corn to Britain.

Canada, overshadowed by her powerful neighbour, developed much more slowly than the USA. She also remained loyal to Britain and provided her with troops in the Boer War and in the two World Wars.

A penal settlement

The British originally chose Australia as a penal settlement. The first contingent of 'transported' criminals landed in Botany Bay in 1788. However, it did not take the authorities long to appreciate Australia's potential as a settlement colony. In 1797, Merino sheep and cattle were introduced, and they flourished. By 1815, 'squatters' were carving out great estates in New South Wales in south-eastern Australia, the original area of settlement.

The vast size of Australia soon led to the creation of a number of new colonies: Tasmania in 1812; Western Australia in 1829; and South Australia in 1836. The original colony of New South Wales was further subdivided to give rise to Victoria in 1851 and Queensland in 1859. At first, the governor had absolute powers, but from 1843 onwards there was a gradual move towards responsible government. The Australian Colonies Act of 1850 gave the colonies more power by allowing them to establish their own constitutions.

The Gold Rush

Although the transportation of convicts to Australia continued until 1853 (1866 in the case of Western Australia), the main reason for the rapid increase in the colonies' population was large scale immigration from Britain. Settlement in Australia was encouraged by colonization schemes like Gibbon Wakefield's in South Australia in 1834, and by the British Poor Law Unions, who were only too happy to finance the emigration of paupers to the colonies. Inspired by the resemblance between the hills and valleys of California and the Blue Mountains in New South Wales, a farmer called Hargraves set out in search of gold. He found deposits of the metal in the foothills of the Blue Mountains. Later, much more important finds were made in Victoria and a full-scale gold rush took place. These discoveries encouraged a large upsurge in immigration, which meant that many aborigines, the original peoples of Australia who led a nomadic existence, were expelled from their hunting grounds.

Federation

At first, the British had valued Australia only as a supply base for India, but due to the great advances in maritime transport it quickly came to have a much greater importance for the mother country. First, the introduction of 'clipper' sailing ships and then steamers significantly reduced the sailing time between the two countries. Britain began to import large quantities of wool from Australia and then, with

Opposite *Australia was originally used by Britain as a land for the resettlement of convicts.*

the invention of refrigeration, vast quantities of meat.

Fear of the German and Japanese advance in the Pacific, as well as internal difficulties over tariff duties and inter-state railways, forced the Australians to consider federation. In 1900, the Commonwealth of Australia Act created a federal government, although the individual states retained considerable powers.

Prospectors washing gold in Australia. The discovery of the metal encouraged increasing numbers of immigrants to the country.

Mustering sheep in Australia. Large quantities of wool were exported to Britain.

New Zealand

Britain's connection with New Zealand began in 1790 when Captain Cook visited the islands. But from that moment until the 1830s, the only European visitors were sealers and whalers. In 1839, however, Gibbon Wakefield started systematic colonization. In consequence, Britain annexed New Zealand in 1840. The governor promptly made the Treaty of Waitangi with the Maori chiefs, guaranteeing them their lands in return for recognizing British rule. The Maori people had been living in New Zealand long before the Europeans arrived. This treaty imposed a strong moral obligation on the British government to safeguard the rights of the Maoris.

However, relations between the white settlers and the Maoris soon deteriorated and the first Maori War took place in 1845–6. Sir George Grey was sent out to settle the affair, which he did with great speed. One of the most important measures he took was to divide New Zealand into six provinces, each with an elected council. Between 1847 and 1860, the white population doubled as immigration boomed, but, as on the Great Plains of America, the settlers wanted the lands belonging to the native peoples. The Maoris again rose in revolt from

The surrender of the Tauranga natives in 1864. The British colonization of New Zealand brought her into conflict with the Maoris.

1860–69 and Sir George Grey had to be recalled to solve the problem. Trust was gradually restored by giving the Maoris direct representation in the New Zealand Parliament, which replaced the provincial councils in 1876.

New Zealand's fortune was also made by advances in methods of transportation and refrigeration. This enabled her to become one of Britain's main suppliers of meat and dairy produce. The New Zealanders, however, were fiercely independent and refused to enter the Australian Commonwealth in 1900.

Throughout the nineteenth century both Australia and New Zealand maintained close ties with Britain, receiving most of their immigrants and their capital investment from the mother country. They also continued to benefit from the protection of the Royal Navy and supported the British in both World Wars.

6 THE CONQUEST OF THE STEPPES

Until 1800 most Europeans regarded the Russians as barbarians, but after their important contribution to the defeat of Napoleon I, in 1815, the rest of Europe became aware of the potential of this rapidly growing state. In the eighteenth century, Russians had explored the Arctic and established settlements on the American coast. They had also colonized the northern shores of the Black Sea. In the nineteenth century they pushed out from their power base in Europe in an obsessive search for new territory and for greater resources. This was the result partly of a rapidly increasing population and partly of the government's attempt to divert people's attention from its disastrous foreign and domestic policy. According to one historian, 'The imperial advance of Russia was definitely adopted as a substitute for reform at home.'

In the south, the Russians conquered the Caucasus, Azerbaijan, Georgia and Armenia between 1839 and 1859. Masses of Cossacks – people of mixed origin from the southern frontier regions – Russians and Volga Germans flooded into these new lands and started cultivating wheat and raising sheep. In the twentieth century Baku became the centre of the Russian oil industry and Chiatura became a huge producer of manganese.

Russian imperial expansion extended southwards into areas such as Georgia, where settlers cultivated the land for wheat.

The Crimean War

The Russians also sought to push south into the Balkans. The Tsars of Russia believed themselves to be the heirs to the Byzantine Empire, which had dominated the straits between the Black and Mediterranean Seas, and they also saw themselves as the main supporters of the Orthodox Church. For many years, the Ottoman Turks had blocked any advance in the Balkans, but, the Turkish Empire was now in full decline and the Tsar hoped to be able to exploit its weaknesses. However, when Russian aggression led to the outbreak of the Crimean War in 1854, the British, French and Austrians supported the Turks. After a series of badly-handled battles, the corrupt Turkish Empire was preserved and Russian ambitions thwarted (see also page 61).

The Siege of Sebastopol in 1855 in the Crimean War. Intervention by the Great Powers halted Russian aggression against the Ottomans.

*The Trans-Siberian Railway enabled the Russians to extend control
eastwards to the Pacific coast.*

Central Asia

Undeterred by this setback, the Russians occupied Kazakhstan, the
land between the Ural Mountains and Lake Balkhash. This enormous
area was the home of nomadic pastoralists who, with their flocks and
herds, followed age-old routes. They too were pushed aside by incoming Russian farmers, who fenced off grazing land like their contem-
poraries in the American West.

The Russians then turned to Turkestan, which lies to the south of
Kazakhstan and extends from the eastern shores of the Caspian Sea
westwards to the frontier of China. This land contained famous centres
of ancient civilization like Tashkent and Samarkand. At the time of
conquest, the area was still divided into the Khanates, of Khiva,
Bukhara and Kholand. Khiva and Bukhara were subjugated between
1864 and 1868, while Kholand was occupied in the 1870s. Although the
new Russian settlers grew much needed cotton crops, they remained
small farmers, greatly burdened by debt.

All along their huge southern frontier, the Russians wielded great
influence and their spies penetrated deep into Turkish Armenia,
Persia, Afghanistan and Kashmir. The British deeply resented their
presence in the last three countries, which threatened her position in
India. Further to the east, the Russians clashed with the Chinese and
Japanese because of their activities in Mongolia and Manchuria. The
last quarter of the nineteenth century witnessed a series of serious
incidents along this frontier that threatened to bring about a full scale
war between the Great Powers.

41

The Conquest of Siberia

Further to the north, the Russians steadily advanced across the vast spaces of Siberia. Originally sparsely populated by tribes of wandering Ostyaks, Tungus and Yakuts, this area greatly attracted Russian serfs seeking freedom from the oppressive feudal system. Officially, the occupation was purely a military one, but by the 1890s the Russian government was encouraging peasants to settle in this area. In 1860, the Pacific Coastal Province was annexed and the port of Vladivostock was opened. Russian control of this vast area was confirmed by the building of the Trans-Caspian (1883–6) and the Trans-Siberian (1891–1904) Railways.

The Manchurian crisis

The Russians were by no means satisfied with these colossal gains. Vladivostock was an unsuitable base for their Pacific fleet, because it was closed by ice for several months during the winter. The Russians coveted the Chinese provinces of Manchuria and Korea, which had both rich mineral deposits and ice-free ports. Although Manchu China was weak and could offer little resistance, Russian ambitions conflicted with those of Japan. The Russians carefully cultivated good relations with China and signed a treaty of friendship with her in 1896. In 1898, the Russians 'persuaded' the Chinese to lease them Port Arthur on the Manchurian coast and to agree to it being linked by rail to the Trans-Siberian Railway. The Japanese were furious at the Russian advance. Relations worsened when the Russians occupied the whole of Manchuria in 1900.

The Russo-Japanese war

Meanwhile the domestic situation in Russia had steadily declined. There had been serious rioting not only in the countryside but also in the new urban industrial areas. The government feared that unless something diverted its people from the appalling domestic conditions there would be a revolution. Many counsellors felt that 'a small war' would serve such a purpose, and so the Russians deliberately allowed tension to mount between the Japanese and themselves. When the Russo-Japanese War of 1904–5 broke out, the Russians quickly discovered that they had greatly underestimated the power of the Japanese. The Russian Grand Fleet was sunk at the Battle of Tshushima and the Russian army was defeated at the Siege of Mukden. Revolution broke out in St Petersburg and Moscow, and the Tsar was forced to make peace with Japan.

Opposite *Russians defending Port Arthur on the Manchurian coast, which was in a strategically vital position.*

The Russian defeat in the Battle of Tsushima at the hands of the Japanese led to the 1905 revolution in Russia.

The Berlin to Baghdad Railway

While the Tsars had been concentrating on the Far East, the Germans had been 'invading' some of Russia's oldest spheres of influence. Kaiser William II visited Turkey in 1898 and greatly increased German influence there. The most important concession he obtained was permission to build the Berlin-Constantinople-Baghdad Railway. This scheme, which would provide the shortest route to India and the Far East from Europe threatened both Russian and British interests in the Middle East. Common fear of Germany led to an improvement in Russo-British relations. The two Great Powers agreed on separate spheres of influence in Persia and together with France formed the Triple Entente in 1907.

The expansion of Russia eastwards and the USA westwards towards the Pacific followed much the same pattern in the nineteenth century. Both had to subjugate native peoples and to introduce millions of new settlers. They also had to build railways to link their lands together. However, Russia was not strong or efficient enough to exploit these lands to the full. This feat was achieved by the Russian communists between the two World Wars.

7 JEWELS OF THE EAST

India and South East Asia were the scene of feverish imperial advances during the nineteenth century. Rivalry in the Far East involved the European powers and also the USA, Russia and Japan.

British reforms in India

The British East India Company, a trading organization, conquered the massive sub-continent of India in approximately eighty years after 1757. Revenue was collected regularly and the huge Indian market was opened to British goods. Among the reforms introduced by Lord William Bentinck, Governor-General from 1828 to 1835, was the suppression of the Hindu custom of suttee, the burning of a widow on her husband's pyre. He also eliminated thuggee, the practice of ritual murder in the name of the goddess Kali. He was determined to instil British ideas: 'General education is my panacea for the regeneration of India', he wrote. English became the state language and roads, canals and, later, railways were built. Bentinck even involved some Indians in his administration by appointing them as judges.

The Indian Mutiny in 1857 forced the British government to change its policy and to take over government of India.

The demand for expensive teak and the need to defend India led to the Burmese campaigns of 1826 and 1852. These resulted in the annexation of Lower Burma. This move was also a reply to the build-up of French influence in nearby Indo-China. Defence of the northern frontiers led to wars with the Sikhs and Afghans. In 1846, the British took over the Punjab. However, the Sikhs rose in revolt in 1848–9 and accepted British rule only after a bitterly fought campaign.

The Indian Mutiny
The reforming activities of the governor-generals created considerable tension in India. The situation was not helped by the flooding of the Indian market with British cloth, which ruined millions of Indian handloom weavers. The army became restive when it was employed overseas, but the most serious cause for complaint was the introduction of new cartridges greased with animal fat. This was unacceptable to Hindu and Muslim alike, for whom cows and pigs respectively were sacred animals. Although the cartridges were withdrawn, the harm had been done and the sepoys rose in revolt at Meerut on 10 May 1857. The authorities were unprepared and for a time the situation was serious, with Delhi, Cawnpore and Lucknow besieged. However, the peoples of Southern India, the Deccan and the Punjab did not join the revolt. When British reinforcements arrived they took a savage revenge for the atrocities committed by the mutineers.

The proclamation of Queen Victoria as Empress of India at Delhi in 1877 heralded a new age of British rule in the country.

An Indian infantry regiment led by British officers. The Indian army helped to defend British interests in the Indian sub-continent.

The Raj

The Mutiny caused Britain to take the management of India out of the hands of the East India Company, and to govern it directly. Later, in 1877, Queen Victoria was proclaimed Empress of India, delegating her power to a viceroy and a council, which contained some Indian aristocrats. The British made special efforts to win the support of the Indian princes, who they thought would support the British Raj or administration. From 1857 onwards, far less pressure was exerted on the Indians to accept Western culture. Indeed, after the publication of the Indian Penal Code in 1861, there were no more social reforms until the First World War. Despite this many Indians remained dissatisfied, and Hindus set up the Indian National Congress Party in 1885. The British government tried to satisfy some of their ambitions with the Morley-Minto reforms of 1906. The Imperial Legislative Council was enlarged to include a number of elected representatives while Indians were appointed to serve on each province's executive council. The large Indian Army was used by Britain in her imperial adventures and in the First World War. It enabled Britain to become a military power comparable to France or Germany.

47

French Indo-China

French interest in South East Asia can be traced back to the seventeenth century, but their fierce appetite for colonies in this area was greatly increased by defeat in the Franco-Prussian War of 1870–71. French Indo-China consisted of Cochin China (1862), Cambodia (1863), Annam (1883), Tongking (1884) and Laos (1893). The British envied France's success and promptly annexed Upper Burma in 1886 as 'compensation'. When the French started to exert pressure on Siam, increasing tension between the two Great Powers led to the Mekong Incident in 1893. As in the case of the Fashoda Incident in Africa, war was avoided only at the last moment. The Siamese sensibly accepted aid from both powers and quickly transformed their country into a modern state.

Sir Stamford Raffles, the colonial administrator, obtained the islands of Java, Sumatra and Singapore for Britain.

Under British rule Singapore became one of the world's most important commercial centres.

Malaya

To the south of Indo-China, Sir Stamford Raffles, on behalf of the British East India Company, seized the Dutch islands of Java and Sumatra in 1810. During his rule, torture was forbidden, slavery discouraged and taxes lightened. In 1819, he obtained Singapore, which he made a great centre for commerce. In 1824, Britain resigned her claims to Java and Sumatra in return for the port of Malacca. Penang, Singapore and Malacca were united to form the Straits Settlements. Originally, the British had been attracted to this area by the need to protect their sea route to China, but later tin mining and rubber plantations created great wealth. Many Chinese people migrated to the area with British encouragement. Gradually, the British spread their influence throughout the Malay peninsula until the Federal State of Malaya was created in 1895 under the rule of a British resident general.

Borneo and New Guinea

Borneo was another target for the imperial powers. In 1841, a Briton called James Brook was made Rajah of Sarawak by the ruler of Brunei as a reward for his outstanding services. He and his successors remained independent rulers until Sarawak became a British colony in 1946. During the 1870s, British traders successfully penetrated the province of Sabah in northern Borneo. Papua-New Guinea was occupied in 1884–5 and both Sarawak and Sabah became British protectorates in 1888.

The Germans arrived late in South East Asia, but managed to acquire the north coast of New Guinea (King Wilhelm's Land) in 1885 and a group of islands in the Bismarck Archipelago. When British politicians voiced their consternation at these German advances, William Gladstone, the British Prime Minister, replied: 'If Germany is to become a great colonizing power, all I say is, God speed her. She becomes our ally and partner in the great purposes of Providence for the advantage of mankind.' Gladstone shared the view, with many other Christians, that to colonize was to civilize.

The Pacific

The Western Powers' insatiable appetite for colonies led to the annexation of most of the Pacific island groups. Between 1853 and 1906 Britain obtained the Solomon, Fiji, Gilbert and Ellice, and Friendly islands; the French, New Caledonia, part of the New Hebrides and the Loyalty Islands; the Germans, the Marshalls, the Pelews and the Carolines; and the Americans, the Philippines, Guam and Hawaii. These groups of islands had great strategic value and were regarded as centrally important to the defence of China, Japan and the USA.

By 1914, the colonization of India, South East Asia and the Pacific islands was virtually complete. By military might, the European Powers had been able to impose their rule upon peoples of the highest culture as well as so called 'primitives'. These proud peoples deeply resented the high handed treatment they received from their white masters while the sons of their aristocracy were educated in Europe and returned to their homelands determined to obtain at worst, equality and at best, independence. In India there was a growing nationalist movement, although it was not to become a threat for another ten years. Meanwhile the Indian sub-continent was an important part of the European idea of empire.

In 1914, however, white supremacy still seemed to be permanent and invulnerable.

Opposite *Map of South East Asia showing European imperial expansion in the Far East by 1914.*

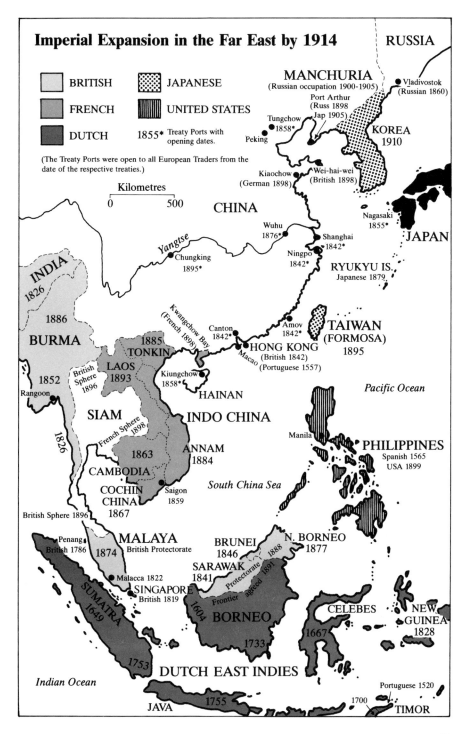

Imperial Expansion in the Far East by 1914

BRITISH   **JAPANESE**

FRENCH   **UNITED STATES**

DUTCH   1855* Treaty Ports with opening dates.

(The Treaty Ports were open to all European Traders from the date of the respective treaties.)

Kilometres
0   500

RUSSIA

MANCHURIA
(Russian occupation 1900-1905)

Vladivostok
(Russian 1860)

Port Arthur
(Russ 1898
Jap 1905)

Tungchow
1858*

Peking

KOREA
1910

Kiaochow
(German 1898)

Wei-hai-wei
(British 1898)

CHINA

Nagasaki
1855*

Wuhu
1876*

Shanghai
1842*

JAPAN

Ningpo
1842*

Yangtse

Chungking
1895*

RYUKYU IS.
Japanese 1879

INDIA
1826

1886

BURMA

Canton
1842*

Amoy
1842*

TAIWAN
(FORMOSA)
1895

Kwangchow Bay
(French 1898)

1885
TONKIN

HONG KONG
(British 1842)
Macao (Portuguese 1557)

Pacific Ocean

British
Sphere
1896

LAOS
1893

Kiungchow
1858*

1852

Rangoon

HAINAN

SIAM

French Sphere 1898

1826

INDO CHINA

Manila

PHILIPPINES
Spanish 1565
USA 1899

1863

ANNAM
1884

CAMBODIA

COCHIN CHINA
1867

Saigon
1859

South China Sea

British Sphere 1896

Penang
British 1786

MALAYA
British Protectorate
1874

Malacca 1822

SINGAPORE
British 1819

SUMATRA
1649

1604

BRUNEI
1846

SARAWAK
1841

Protectorate 1888

1891

N. BORNEO
1877

Frontier agreed

BORNEO

1733

1667

CELEBES

NEW GUINEA
1828

DUTCH EAST INDIES

Indian Ocean

JAVA

1753

1755

1700

Portuguese 1520

TIMOR

8 THE DRAGON AND THE RISING SUN

For centuries, the Chinese and Japanese remained virtually isolated from the rest of the world, regarding foreigners as barbarians. During the nineteenth century, their isolation was brought to a violent and often bloody end.

The First Opium War

Although China sold vast quantities of silk and porcelain to Western Europe, the only substantial item that the Europeans had to offer in exchange was opium. By 1839, there were 2 million addicts in China, and 40,000 chests of opium were being imported annually. When the Emperor Tao-kuang tried to stop the trade, the First Opium War of 1840–42 broke out. The British defeated the Chinese by land and sea, and forced them to sign the Treaty of Nanking by which Canton, Amoy, Foochow, Ningpo and Shanghai were opened to traders and Hong Kong was ceded to Britain. Following this humiliation, the Chinese had to make similar concessions to the USA, Russia, France, Belgium, Norway and Sweden.

Chinese men dyeing and winding silk, one of the luxury items that China shipped out to the West.

A Japanese samurai. Japanese society was highly structured and fiercely resisted the influence of the Great Powers.

Trade with Japan

While the Chinese opened their doors to the 'round eyes', the Japanese continued to lead their traditional way of life. A shogun, who was a military dictator, ruled the country for the sacred but powerless emperor. Japanese society consisted of nobles, samurai (warriors), farmers, artisans and slaves. The peace of this secluded world was shattered in 1853 by the arrival in Tokyo Bay of an American fleet led by Commodore Perry. The Americans wanted to be able to refuel and revictual their ships in Japanese ports as well as trade with the inhabitants. In 1858, the Japanese reluctantly opened five of their ports to American traders. Almost immediately Britain, France, Holland and Russia demanded and obtained similar rights.

The Second Opium War

The Western Powers' actions deeply offended the Chinese and Japanese. The Manchu rulers of China 'lost face' and many of their people took part in the Taiping revolt (1847–64). Worse still, when the Chinese refused to apologize for seizing a British ship, Lord

Palmerston, the British Prime Minister, sent an expeditionary force to capture Canton and Tientsin. When the Chinese refused to surrender, the 'foreign devils' sacked and burnt the beautiful Summer Palace, just outside Peking. On 24 October 1860, British forces entered the Chinese capital and the emperor was compelled to sign the Convention of Peking by which Tientsin was opened to trade and Britain was given Kowloon, a peninsula opposite Hong Kong island.

The Meiji Revolution
The defeats in the Second Opium War convinced many Chinese that their country had to be modernized. The Dowager Empress Tzu-hsi, however, who dominated China from 1870 to her death in 1908, was determined to maintain China's traditional way of life. In spite of her conservatism, European-style arsenals, shipyards, railways and telegraphs were gradually introduced. By contrast, the Japanese were quick to adopt European methods and ideas. The last shogun was deposed in 1868 and the Emperor Meiji (1852–1912) started to rule in person. The Japanese feudal system was abolished and a modern army and navy replaced the proud samurai. Roads, railways and telegraphs were built. A constitution was granted and a western-style education system was created.

In the Second Opium War the Europeans occupied the Summer Palace in Peking, and forced the Chinese to make peace.

Hong Kong, which was acquired by the British from the Chinese, became a vital strategic and commercial centre.

The Sino-Japanese War

Japan rapidly became a military power to be reckoned with. Although the Japanese greatly respected Chinese culture, they coveted parts of her empire, especially Korea and Manchuria. Korea produced rice for export, which would help to feed Japan's increasing population, and Manchuria possessed rich mineral deposits, which Japanese industry needed. In 1876, a Japanese military expedition 'persuaded' the Koreans to sign a commercial treaty. During the years that followed Korea became a Japanese dependency. Eventually, Japan's aggression led to the outbreak of the Sino-Japanese War of 1894–5. The Chinese were easily defeated and made to sign the Treaty of Shimonoseki by which they ceded Formosa and the Liaotung peninsula in Manchuria to Japan as well as paying a large indemnity (compensation). To Japan's fury, Russia, France and Germany intervened and forced her to return Liaotung to China. The Japanese deeply resented this interference, especially when five years later China was persuaded to lease the Liaotung peninsula by the Russians.

55

The Boxer Rising

The unscrupulousness of the European Powers was illustrated by the way they took advantage of China's distress to extract a series of concessions. In 1897 the Germans seized Tsingtao, giving as an excuse the murder of German missionaries in Shantung. In 1898 Kiachow was leased and soon the whole of the vast Shantung peninsula was a German sphere of influence. Not to be outdone, Britain obtained

The first railway in Japan. Once the western Great Powers established themselves in the Far East, Japan was quick to adopt western ideas.

The Foreign Legations in Peking being relieved by forces sent by the Great Powers, after having been besieged by the Boxers.

Wei-hai-wei; France, Kwangchow-wan and Russia, Port Arthur. The Europeans made no attempt to convert the areas around these ports into colonies, because they already dominated China's economic life. Hatred of the 'foreign devils' led to the Boxer Rising in 1900. The Boxers, members of a secret society, massacred many thousands of Chinese converts to Christianity, murdered the German ambassador and tried to drive every European out of China. Even the Foreign Legations in Peking were besieged, but held out with remarkable courage until they were relieved by the combined forces of the Great Powers. The European soldiers in their turn committed terrible atrocities while avenging their dead comrades.

The Boxer Rising ended Tzu-hsi's opposition to westernization. A whole series of reforms were rushed through in an effort to bolster up the decadent Manchu regime. Shortly after the empress's death, however, the monarchy was overthrown in 1911 and Dr Sun Yat-sen became President of the Chinese Republic. The new regime soon collapsed and China had to endure many years of civil war until General Chang Kai-shek and his political party, the Kuomintang, created some kind of stability in the late 1920s.

The Russian army on an arduous march to occupy Manchuria. This action eventually provoked war with Japan.

The Russo-Japanese War

Japan hid her fury over the loss of the Liaotung peninsula, but she did not forget. In 1902, she joined the British in the Anglo-Japanese Alliance. At the same time, the Russians deliberately offended her by occupying the whole of Manchuria. The intense rivalry between the two countries led to the Russo-Japanese War of 1904–5. By the Treaty of Portsmouth, the Russians had to cede the southern half of Sakhalin and Port Arthur to Japan and recognize her control of the disputed area of Korea.

In spite of the pressure exerted by the greedy European Powers, Japan overcame her internal and external problems during the course of the nineteenth century, and, by the start of the First World War, had emerged as a Great Power. China, on the other hand, was still relatively weak although she too had the potential to become one of the most powerful countries in the world. Both countries were attempting to reconcile western ideas and methods with their own rich, traditional cultures.

9 THE EASTERN QUESTION

The so-called Eastern Question revolved around the fate of the Ottoman Empire, particularly in the Balkans. At the beginning of the nineteenth century all the peoples of the Balkans, the Middle East and North Africa were subjects of the once mighty Turks.

A number of European Powers, especially the Russians, Austrians and British, were deeply interested in developments in the Balkans. The Russians regarded themselves as the 'natural protectors' of the Orthodox Christian inhabitants of the area and coveted control of the

Map of the Balkan states in 1914.

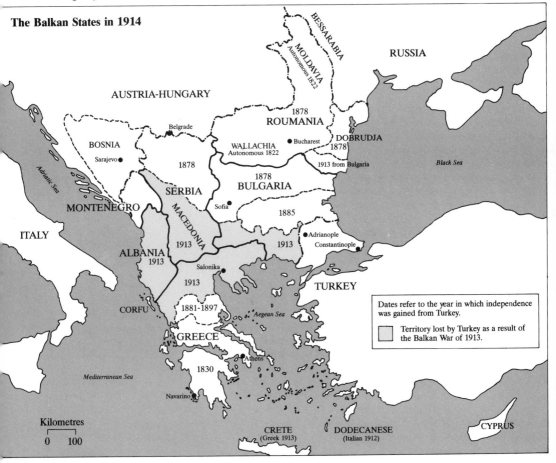

The Balkan States in 1914

RUSSIA

BESSARABIA

MOLDAVIA
Autonomous 1822

AUSTRIA-HUNGARY

1878
ROUMANIA

Belgrade

DOBRUDJA
1878

BOSNIA

Sarajevo

WALLACHIA
Autonomous 1822

Bucharest

1878

1913 from Bulgaria

Black Sea

1878

Adriatic Sea

1878
BULGARIA

SERBIA

MONTENEGRO

MACEDONIA

Sofia

1885

ITALY

Adrianople
Constantinople

ALBANIA
1913

1913

1913

Salonika

1913

TURKEY

CORFU

1881-1897

Aegean Sea

GREECE

1830

Mediterranean Sea

Navarino

Athens

Dates refer to the year in which independence was gained from Turkey.

Territory lost by Turkey as a result of the Balkan War of 1913.

Kilometres

0   100

CRETE
(Greek 1913)

DODECANESE
(Italian 1912)

CYPRUS

Dardanelles and the Bosporus, the straits between the Black and Mediterranean Seas. The Austrians wanted to suppress the growing nationalism of the Slavs already within their empire by absorbing those beyond their frontiers. The British feared that unless the Turks were supported, the Russians would add the Balkans to their empire and threaten British communications with India through the Mediterranean Sea.

The Serbs were the first Balkan people to obtain their freedom. They rose in revolt in 1804–12 and 1815–17 and forced the Turks to grant them autonomy, although they continued to pay tribute to their former rulers. In 1822, the Greeks declared their independence. The Turks responded with the utmost brutality, but the British, French and Russians came to the aid of the Greeks and their combined fleets defeated the Turks at the Battle of Navarino in 1827. Greek independence was recognized by the London Conference of 1830.

Santa Sophia, a great mosque in Constantinople. The Great Powers intervened in the Balkans, claiming to protect Orthodox Christians.

The Russian cavalry preparing to fight in the Caucasus. The Russians aimed to establish supremacy over Turkestan and Kazakhstan.

The Crimean War

The Russians were still determined to partition the Ottoman Empire and seize the Dardanelles and the Bosporus. In 1853, they demanded the right to establish a protectorate over all Orthodox Christians in the Balkans. The Turks, supported by Britain, rejected the ultimatum and declared war. The Russians smashed their way into the Danubian provinces of Moldavia and Wallachia before a combined Anglo-French expedition crossed the Black Sea and invaded the Crimea. The allies forced the Russians to back down and to make peace. The Black Sea was neutralized and Moldavia and Wallachia became autonomous within the Turkish Empire.

The Bulgarian Atrocities

Revolts in Bosnia-Herzgovina and Bulgaria in 1875–6 were put down with horrible brutality. First Serbia and then Russia declared war on the Turks. Russian armies invaded the Caucasus and advanced on Constantinople. By the Treaty of San Stefano in 1878, a 'large' independent Bulgaria was created. This was too much for the British and Austrians who believed the new state would be no more than a Russian satellite. To prevent further warfare, Bismarck, the German Chancellor, acted as an 'honest broker' and convened the Congress of Berlin to discuss the matter. The Congress decided that Bulgaria was to be considerably reduced in size, and recognized the independence of Roumania, Serbia and Montenegro. Russia was to receive Bessarabia; Britain was to receive Cyprus and Austria was to gain administrative control over Bosnia-Herzgovina.

The Treaty of Berlin

The Treaty of Berlin did nothing to resolve Austro-Russian rivalry or to satisfy the aspirations of the Balkan peoples. Indeed, it complicated matters still further as the Germans became intensely interested in developing a 'Germanic wedge' to the Persian Gulf. The idea of the Berlin-to-Baghdad Railway was a symbol of this determination and was as dangerous to Britain and her interests in India as the Russian attempt to seize the straits had been. Bismarck tried to defuse the situation by encouraging the Great Powers to seek success in building up their overseas empires.

The Young Turk Revolution

Only minor adjustments were made to the political geography of the Balkans between 1878 and 1908, the year that the Young Turk revolution broke out. In the aftermath, the Bulgarians declared themselves to be completely independent and Austria annexed Bosnia-Herzgovina. Both Serbia and Russia bitterly opposed the latter move but there was nothing they could do because Germany gave Austria her full support. Nevertheless, the Austrian action was a dangerous one, encouraging the growth of the Pan-Slav movement, which aimed to see all Slav people united in a single state.

Disraeli and Bismarck at the Congress of Berlin, which brought about a temporary halt to Russian designs on the Balkans.

Bulgarian soldiers on the way by rail to the battlefront in the First Balkan War in 1912.

The First Balkan War

Between 1911 and 1912, Turkey's position was weakened still further by war with Italy over Tripoli. By 1912, the Balkan peoples were determined to partition the remaining part of European Turkey among themselves and formed the First Balkan League to prevent Austrian intervention. In October 1912, the League attacked and defeated the Turks. However, the Serbs, backed by the Russians, demanded a land corridor to the Adriatic coastline. This the Austrians strenuously opposed. During the subsequent quarrelling, the Italians tried to take control of the Dodecanese and Albania. This complicated situation was resolved, it appeared, by the Treaty of London in 1913, which declared that Turkey was to be stripped of nearly all her remaining European possessions.

The Second Balkan War

However, the victors could not agree about the division of the spoils and Bulgaria attacked the others with the support of Austria. The Second Balkan League was joined by Roumania, who had been neutral during the first war, and Turkey. Bulgaria was overwhelmed within a month. Austria wanted to go to the aid of her ally, but was persuaded by Germany from taking such a provocative action. The ensuing Treaty of Bucharest was a great disappointment to the Serbs, because continued Austrian opposition denied them access to the Adriatic Sea.

Archduke Franz Ferdinand and his wife about to board their car, shortly before their assassination in Sarajevo.

The Sarajevo crisis

The two wars sharpened the divisions between the Balkan peoples and their patrons among the Great Powers. The Pan-Slavs came to regard the Austrians as their principal enemies. A number of revolutionary secret societies appeared who sought to resolve the deadlock by assassinations. On 28 June 1914, Gavrilo Princip, a member of the secret Young Bosnia Movement, assassinated Archduke Franz Ferdinand, the heir to the Austrian throne, while he was on a state visit to Sarajevo, the Bosnian capital. The complicity of the Serbian government has never been proved and it is extremely unlikely they had anything to do with the plot. However, the Austrians, insisting that the Serbian government was responsible for the plot, delivered an ultimatum. Even though the Serbs agreed to implement most of the demands, the Austrians were not satisfied and declared war on 28 July 1914.

Once 'the unnecessary war' had been launched, the rivalry and mutual suspicions of the Great Powers came home to roost. As a precaution, the Russians partially mobilized their forces – this was necessary as their mobilization scheme was particularly slow. On learning this, the Germans jumped to the conclusion that they were preparing for a full-scale attack and declared war on Russia and France. Soon, Britain was forced to come to the aid of her allies, France and Russia. More and more countries entered the conflict until it truly became the First World War (1914–18).

10 EMPIRES TREMBLE AND FALL

The First World War involved all the Great Powers and many minor powers in a bloody conflict. For four years, Anglo-French and German forces were locked in battle along the Western Front. The Italo-Austrian Front remained almost as static for most of the war. After a short flourish of activity in 1915 the war on the Balkan Front also reached stalemate. Only the Eastern Front witnessed a war of rapid movement, illustrating the changes of fortune enjoyed by the Russians and their Germano-Austrian opponents. Even the Turks managed to fend off a determined Anglo-French attack on the Dardanelles, the strait separating European and Asian Turkey.

Allied forces in the Dardanelles on what was to be the unsuccessful Gallipoli campaign in 1915.

The Colonial Fronts

By comparison with what was going on in Europe, events in the colonies were relatively low key affairs. The South Africans overran German South West Africa without much difficulty. German Togo and Cameroon were easily occupied by Anglo-French forces. The story in German East Africa was very different, however. General Paul von Lettow led the British forces a merry dance and remained undefeated when the armistice was signed. Anglo-French agents were particularly successful in exploiting Arab nationalism and in stimulating a series of revolts against the Ottoman Turks in Arabia, Palestine and Syria. But Britain's attempt to secure the Persian Gulf oil fields from Turkey led to the bitterly fought Mesopotamian campaign.

T. E. Lawrence (second row, second from right) and Arab nationalist leaders, who greatly helped the Allied cause in the Middle East.

Tsar Nicholas II and his wife Alexandra, who failed to stem the revolutionary tide in Russia and had to abdicate in 1917.

The Russian Revolution
By 1917, both the Central Powers and the Allies were exhausted. In March, Tsar Nicholas II was forced to abdicate and Russia became a republic. Following another series of crushing defeats, the Bolsheviks carried out a revolution in November and made peace with the Germans in 1918. This might have been a fatal blow for the Allies, if the USA had not joined them in 1917. When the 1918 German spring offensive failed and the Allies counter-attacked, the Central Powers had to negotiate a series of armistices during October and November to bring an end to the war.

Collapsing empires
The First World War brought four of the old empires crashing down. The Central Powers were humiliated. Germany lost Alsace-Lorraine to France, West Prussia to Poland, the Saar Basin was handed over to the League of Nations for fifteen years and the Rhineland was occupied by Allied troops. All Germany's overseas empire was taken from

her and she was compelled to pay massive reparations for the 'damage' she had caused. The Hapsburg empire was dismantled. Austria and Hungary became small land-locked countries, having had their imperial provinces taken away to become the new states of Czechoslovakia and Yugoslavia. While Russia survived revolution, invasion and civil war virtually intact, and retained her Asiatic conquests, the old Romanov empire in Europe was lost: Poland, Esthonia, Latvia, Lithuania and Finland became independent states. The Ottoman Sultanate survived until 1922 before giving way to the Republic of Turkey. The Turkish empire was taken over by the Allies or became independent. France took responsibility for Syria and the Lebanon, and Britain for Palestine and Iraq; the British also wielded great influence in Jordan and Arabia.

The Far East
In the Far East, the Japanese had been quick to join the Allies in 1916. This enabled them to play a prominent part in the conquest of the German concessions in China and their Pacific dependencies. The Chinese, by contrast, were slow to appreciate what was happening and did not join the Allies early enough to thwart Japan's ambitions. The rest of the European Powers' Far Eastern colonies remained apparently unaffected. However, the news of the collapse of old empires was

The seizure of power by the Bolsheviks in the 1917 Russian Revolution led to the Russians making an early peace with Germany in 1918.

The British Prime Minister Lloyd George signing the Treaty of Versailles, which concluded the First World War.

significant in encouraging nationalism and hopes of autonomy. The undermining of European prestige was begun by the First and completed by the Second World War (1939–45). However, for the time being, Europeans remained in charge of colossal empires in Africa and the Near, Middle and Far East.

Imperial patterns
The reasons behind the creation of empires between 1815 and 1918 were both varied and complex. It has been suggested that 'imperialism may best be seen as the extension of the political struggle in Europe'. While this certainly was a factor, of equal if not greater importance was the desire to control sources of raw materials and to compete for the world's markets as more and more countries industrialized. Russia and the USA, as part of large physical landmasses, were able to consolidate their conquests into single huge states. However, the empires of Britain, France and Germany could not be integrated with the mother country in the same way, and were so disparate and far-flung across the world that effective government was difficult. Competition between the Great Powers for colonies contributed to a sense of distrust and fear, and provided a hostile background in which war broke out in 1914.

DATE CHART

1776–83 The American War of Independence ended Britain's first great empire.

1789– 1804 The Revolutionary Wars spread the idea of nationalism throughout Europe.

1815 The Treaty of Vienna ended the Napoleonic Wars (1804–15).

1820 Congress of Troppau: the Great Powers agreed to defeat nationalism through co-operation and intervention.

1830 A year of revolutions in France, Belgium, the German Confederation, Italy, Switzerland and Poland.

1840 Britain annexed New Zealand.

1839–42 The First Opium War between Britain and China.

1848 A year of revolutions in Italy, Germany, Austria, Hungary, Belgium, Switzerland and France.

1849 The California Gold Rush.

1853 Commodore Perry forcibly ended Japan's years of isolation.

1854–6 The Crimean War.

1857 The Indian Mutiny.

1861 Victor Emmanuel proclaimed King of Italy.

1866 The Austro-Prussian War: Prussia united northern Germany.

1867 The British North America Act enabled the Canadians to set up a federation.

1869 The Suez Canal opened.

1860s & 70s The French take over Indo-China; the Russians absorb the Caucasus, Turkestan and Siberia; the Americans conquer the West.

1870 Diamonds discovered in Griqualand.

1870–71 Franco-Prussian War: German Empire and the Third French Republic founded.

1875–6 The Bulgarian Atrocities led to a Balkan crisis.

1878 The Congress of Berlin settled the Balkan problem and triggered off a decade of frantic colonization.

1880–81 The First Boer War;

Britain defeated.

1884–9 Germany obtained Togoland, the Cameroon, South West Africa and Tanganyika.

1893 The Mekong Incident; both Britain and France wanted control of Siam.

1895–6 The Jameson Raid: an attempt to overthrow the Transvaal government miscarried.

1898 The Fashoda Incident: France and Britain clashed over control of the Sudan.

1899–1902 The Second Boer war.

1900 The Commonwealth of Australia Act; the Boxer Rising in China.

1904–5 The Russo-Japanese War.

1908 The Young Turk Revolution.

1910 The Union of South Africa.

1911 The Chinese Revolution – the end of the Manchu dynasty.

1912 The First Balkan War.

1913 The Second Balkan War.

1914 The Sarajevo Crisis; the Panama Canal opened.

1914–18 The First World War.

1917 The Russian Revolution – the Romanov dynasty fell.

1918 The Armistice – the Hohenzollern and Hapsburg dynasties fell.

1922 The Ottoman Sultanate ended; Turkish Republic set up.

GLOSSARY

Abdicate   To renounce a throne.

Alliance   The joining together by treaty of two or more countries for military purposes.

Annex   To take over territory by conquest or occupation.

Armistice   A truce while the terms of a peace treaty are being worked out.

Autonomy   Self-government.

Bolshevik   A member of the Russian Social Democratic Party.

Central Powers   The First World War alliance of Germany, Austria, Bulgaria and Turkey.

Colony   A territory that has been officially acquired by another state.

Congress   A meeting of national representatives.

Constituent assembly   A meeting of delegates to draw up a constitution.

Constitution   The principles, rules and methods by which a state is governed.

Dollar diplomacy   An American way of controlling other countries' policies by the giving or withholding of financial aid.

Dynastic struggles   The rivalry of opposing royal families for gain.

Dominion   A self-governing member of the British Commonwealth of nations.

Emigration   The movement of people from their mother country to another land.

Entente   A friendly understanding or an alliance without binding military clauses.

Executive council   A group of people delegated to govern a district or province of a colony.

Federation   A political union in which power is shared between several states or provinces and a federal government.

Feudal system   A hierarchical society ruled by a small military caste, which is supported by a very large class of peasants.

Great Power   In the nineteenth century the Great Powers were Britain, France, Russia, Prussia (later Germany), Austria, the USA and Japan. They could be called great in terms of their political influence, resources and military strength.

Hindus   Members of one of the world's religions who believe in gods, the transmigration of souls and nirvana.

Immigration The entry of settlers into a new country.

Legations The official residences of diplomatic representatives.

Legislative council A group of people who are delegated by the mother country to make laws for a colony.

Monroe Doctrine A principle of US foreign policy that opposes the influence or intervention of outside powers in the Americas.

Mormons The members of an American religious sect founded by Joseph Smith in 1830.

Muslims Members of a religion who believe that there is one god, Allah, whose prophet was Muhammad.

Nationalism A belief that the members of a nation or race should be united to form one country.

Oligarchy A small body of individuals ruling a state.

Orthodox Christians The Eastern branch of the Catholic Church, which is ruled by Patriarchs instead of the Pope.

Pan-Slav movement: A political group determined to unite all the Balkan Slavs in one state.

Protectorate A territory placed under the protection of a Great Power without being included within its empire.

Reparations The compensation the Central Powers were ordered to pay the Allies for damage inflicted during the First World War.

Responsible government A political system by which the government is made responsible to the people, usually through elections.

Republic A state where the supreme power rests with the people's representatives and the executive is a president.

Satellite A state which is completely subordinate to a Great Power.

Sepoys Indian soldiers.

Social Darwinism The idea that only the strongest can survive.

Steppes The great Russian grasslands.

Tariffs Duties or customs payable on the importing or exporting of goods.

Treaty A formal agreement between two or more countries.

Tribute Money paid by subject peoples to their prince or state.

Ultimatum A formal set of demands under threat of war.

Viceroy A governor acting with royal authority in a colony.

FURTHER READING

Blackwood, Alan *Spotlight on the Rise of Modern China* (Wayland, 1986)

Chamberlain, M. E. *The New Imperialism* (Historical Association Pamphlet G73)

Fieldhouse, D. K. *The Colonial Empires* (Macmillan, 1982)

Gibson, Michael *Spotlight on the Collapse of Empires* (Wayland, 1986)

Gibson, Michael *Spotlight on the First World War* (Wayland, 1985)

Kiernan, V. G. *European Empires from Conquest to Collapse 1815–1960* (Fontana, 1982)

Symonds, P. *Britain, Europe and the World 1714–1848* (Heinemann, 1975)

Taylor, A. J. P. *The Struggle for Mastery in Europe 1848–1918* (OUP, 1971)

Apart from these general studies, the reader should seek information from outline histories of individual countries or studies of the world's great leaders.

PICTURE ACKNOWLEDGEMENTS

The illustrations were supplied by: The Bridgeman Art Library *cover*; BBC Hulton Picture Library 27, 32, 41, 47, 65, 66; Mary Evans Picture Library 8, 9, 10, 13, 14, 15, 18, 19, 20, 23, 24, 25, 26, 28, 30, 31, 33, 34, 36, 37, 38, 39, 40, 43, 44, 45, 48, 49, 52, 53, 54, 55, 61, 62, 67, 68; The Mansell Collection 11, 16, 21, 22, 29, 46, 58, 63, 64, 69; Malcolm Walker 17, 51, 59; Wayland Picture Library 56, 57, 60.

INDEX